# FACING YOUR FEARS

# FACING YOUR FEAR OF SNAKES

BY NICOLE A. MANSFIELD

PEBBLE
a capstone imprint

Published by Pebble, an imprint of Capstone
1710 Roe Crest Drive, North Mankato, Minnesota 56003
capstonepub.com

Library of Congress Cataloging-in-Publication Data is available on the Library of Congress website.
ISBN: 9780756574345 (hardcover)
ISBN: 9780756574079 (paperback)
ISBN: 9780756574307 (ebook PDF)

Summary: Describes the reasons for fearing snakes and simple tips to overcome these fears.

Editorial Credits
Editor: Erika L. Shores; Designer: Heidi Thompson; Media Researcher: Jo Miller; Production Specialist: Tori Abraham

Image Credits
Alamy: imageBROKER, 5; Associated Press: Martin Mejia, 9; Getty Images: Compassionate Eye Foundation/Shalom Ormsby, Cover, Hero Images, 11; Shutterstock: Aksenova Natalya (glue), 20, AleksandraAv, 16, Bildagentur Zoonar GmbH, 7, Carlos wild, 13, Domira (background), cover and throughout, HABRDA, 19, JGA, 15, Kapitosh (cloud), cover and throughout, komkrit Preechachanwate, 6, Lisa Crawford, 4, liza1979 (paper, scissors), 20, Marish (brave girl), cover and throughout, Mega Pixel (google eyes), 21, pixelheadphoto digitalskillet, 17, SaGa Studio (leaves), 21

All internet sites appearing in back matter were available and accurate when this book was sent to press.

Printed and bound in China.  PO5377

# TABLE OF CONTENTS

Words in **bold** are in the glossary.

# FEAR OF SNAKES

They slither. They're silent. Snakes slink along the ground. A lot of people are scared of snakes. Are you?

Let's learn more about snakes and how they act. Find out what to do if you see one. You can learn to handle your fear.

# ALL ABOUT SNAKES

Snakes are cold-blooded. Their body temperature depends on their surroundings. Snakes lie on rocks in the sun to warm up. They hide in grasses to cool off.

Snakes are an important part of the food chain. They eat mice, lizards, and insects. Without snakes, the numbers of these small animals can grow too large in an area.

Many people fear snakes with **fangs**. These kinds of snakes are **venomous**. Venom is a liquid poison. It squirts out of their teeth when they bite. The venom helps snakes kill the animals they eat.

Some snakes have heads shaped like triangles. Their mouths may bulge. This is because they have **sacs** inside that hold venom.

# SNAKE BEHAVIOR

It is important to be careful around all snakes. Even snakes without venom can bite.

Sometimes a snake plays dead when it feels unsafe. Its body will look limp. The snake may flip onto its back. The snake is pretending. It could still attack.

Snakes feel unsafe when bigger animals or people get too close. A scared snake may wrap and stack its body on top of itself. This is called coiling. A coiled snake's next move may be to jump out and bite.

Some snakes may rattle their tails. This is a warning. It means you are too close.

# SNAKE SAFETY

Snakes often hide in tall grasses. Snakes also hang out in bushes, rocks, and quiet corners. When outside, wear shoes that cover your toes. Sneakers keep your feet safe if you accidentally step on a snake.

Stomp your feet when you walk. It creates **vibrations**. Snakes on the ground feel you coming. They will slither away fast.

If you come across a snake, you might jump or scream. Your heart might beat fast. It is normal to react this way. You were **startled**.

If a snake startles you, take a deep breath. Stay still. Then slowly back away from the snake. As soon as you can, tell an adult.

Remember that snakes want to be left alone. Never pick up or throw rocks at snakes. Stay away from places where they hang out. Knowing what to do around snakes will help you stay calm and feel brave.

# MAKE A LEAF SNAKE

Make your own snake using leaves. Take your snake outside to hide in the grass or lie in the sun.

## What You Need

- 8 to 10 leaves
- glue
- googly eyes
- red paper or fabric
- scissors

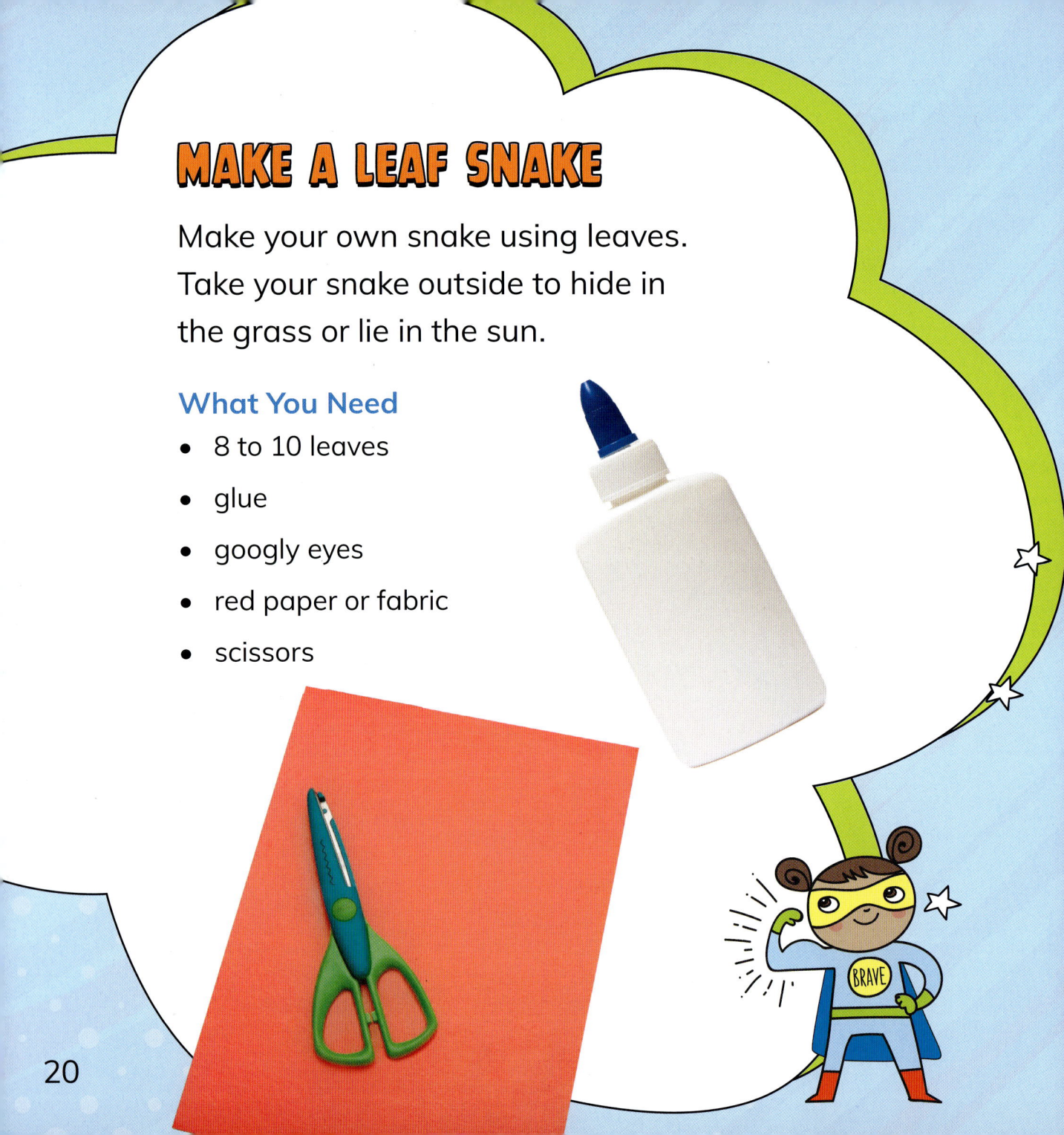

## What You Do

1. Lay out the leaves in the shape of a giant letter "S." Each leaf should overlap the next one.

2. Glue the overlapping leaves together so they form a long S-shaped snake.

3. Glue two googly eyes onto your snake's head.

4. Cut a small piece of red paper or fabric into a rectangle.

5. Cut a small V-shape into the end of the rectangle to make a forked tongue for your snake.

6. Glue the forked tongue to the end of your snake's head.

# GLOSSARY

**fang** (FANG)—a clawlike tooth that squirts out venom

**sac** (SAK)—a part of a plant or animal that is shaped like a pocket or bag

**startle** (STAHRT-uhl)—to move or jump suddenly in surprise or fright

**venomous** (VEN–uh–mis)—having or making poison

**vibration** (VYE-bray-shun)—a trembling motion

## READ MORE

Austin, Joy. *Snakes in My Garden*. Tampa, FL: BeaLu Books, 2020.

Duling, Kaitlyn. *12 Phobias About Living Things*. Mankato, MN: 12-Story Library, 2021.

Walker, Alan. *Ouch! Snakes that Bite*. New York: Crabtree Publishing, 2022.

## INTERNET SITES

*Ball Python*
youtube.com/watch?v=xkvHg8oZ-YA

*Snake Facts and Information*
nationalgeographic.com/animals/reptiles/facts/snakes-1

# INDEX

# ABOUT THE AUTHOR

Nicole A. Mansfield is a wife, mother and educator. She dedicates this book to the people who have taught her the most, her family—Connie, Walter, and Cheryl Mills, Justin, Victorious, Justine, and Zion Mansfield. Nicole is passionate about serving at her church and vacationing at the beach!